John Wall

By Jon M. Fishman

AMAZING ATHLETES

Lerner Publications ◆ Minneapolis

Lerner Publications Company
A division of Lerner Publishing Group, Inc.
241 First Avenue North
Minneapolis, MN 55401 USA

For reading levels and more information, look up this title at www.lernerbooks.com.

Library of Congress Cataloging-in-Publication Data

Fishman, Jon M.
    John Wall / by Jon M. Fishman.
        pages cm
    Includes index.
        ISBN 978-1-4677-9404-6 (lb : alk. paper) — ISBN 978-1-4677-9405-3 (pb : alk. paper) —
    ISBN 978-1-4677-9407-7 (eb pdf)
        1. Wall, John, 1990– 2. Basketball players—United States—Biography—Juvenile literature.
    I. Title.
    GV884.C88F56 2016
    796.323092—dc23 [B]   2015013889

Manufactured in the United States of America
1 – BP – 7/15/15

TABLE OF CONTENTS

John Wall (*right*) shoots over Mo Williams of the Charlotte Hornets.

MAGIC ON THE COURT

Just three seconds remained in **overtime**. The game was tied, 101–101. Washington Wizards **point guard** John Wall jumped off the court and released a 19-foot shot. *Clang!* The ball smacked the **rim** and bounced away as time ran out. The game was headed to a second overtime!

John and the Wizards were playing against the Charlotte Hornets on March 27, 2015. Washington had lost four games in a row. They wanted to beat the Hornets and get back on a winning path.

John dribbles past Kemba Walker in the first half of the game.

In the second overtime, John knocked down the first basket for Washington. Then teammate Marcin Gortat scored. But the Hornets were keeping pace. The game was tied again, 105–105.

John is one of the top passers in the NBA. The year before, he had the second most **assists** per game (8.8) in the NBA for the season.

John goes in for a layup.

His passes help teammates get open shots all around the court. But John is also one of the league's top scorers. With barely more than two minutes to go in the second overtime, he took a shot from beyond the **three-point line**. *Swish!* Then he sank a 15-foot shot for two points. Charlotte couldn't keep up. Washington won the game, 110–107.

John shoots in the double-overtime game against the Charlotte Hornets.

The Verizon Center is the Wizards' home arena.

In 2015, John and his teammates visited the White House. John even got to shoot baskets with President Obama!

The Wizards had struggled during John's first few years with the team. But in 2014–2015, the team had a winning record for the second year in a row. And for the second time, the fans voted for John to play in the All-Star Game.

John's talent and years of practice had made him one of the best basketball players in the world.

John helped the Wizards achieve their 2014–2015 winning record.

Raleigh, North Carolina, is a city of more than 431,000 people.

LIFE LESSONS

Johnathan Wall Jr. was born on September 6, 1990, in Raleigh, North Carolina. He lived with his father, John Wall, and his mother, Frances Pulley. John Jr. has a younger sister and an older brother and sister.

When John was about one year old, his father stole money from a store. John Sr. went to prison. On weekends, John and his younger sister, Cierra, traveled with their mother to visit John Sr. The boy loved his father and wanted him all to himself. But he had to share his time with his sister. Each weekend, the family could spend only one or two hours together. "We could hug," John said. "We could touch and everything."

John laughs with his sisters Tonya (*center*) and Cierra (*far right*).

When John wasn't in school or visiting his father, he was playing basketball. He had a basketball hoop small enough to allow him to **dunk**. He dunked so often that he broke the hoop. "[It seemed] like every week . . . I would have to go buy another one," Frances said. John also shot baskets with friends at nearby Roberts Park.

As a child, John worried that he might not grow tall enough for the NBA. "I was always small and skinny . . . so I wondered when I was going to grow," he said.

In 1999, John Sr. was released from prison. He got out one month earlier than scheduled because he was sick. He had cancer, and he wasn't getting any better. John was just happy to have his father back in his life full-time.

That summer, the family took a trip to White Lake, North Carolina. "We stayed on the beach, went on rides, stayed in the water a lot," Frances said. John had a great time. He drew pictures of his family and ate delicious food. But on the last day of the trip, John Sr. became very ill. He was rushed to the hospital and died two days later.

John and his family went to White Lake, North Carolina, for vacation.

After his father's death, John (*center*) used basketball as an outlet for his anger.

LETTING GO

John was sad and angry about his father's death. He didn't understand why people had to die. He began acting out. He treated his sisters unkindly and got into trouble with his friends.

He still loved to play basketball. But John's anger often boiled over on the court.

He would slam the ball down and curse at teammates. "I was mad at everything," John said. "I did not trust coaches, people. Anytime somebody told me something, I just said, 'You don't know what you are talking about.'"

In 2004, John began attending Garner High School. Garner basketball coach Eddie Gray was amazed by John's skill on the court. The young player could shoot from afar or drive to the basket for an easy **layup**. He could also thread the ball between tight spaces to hit teammates with passes.

John's talent was on display when he was able to keep his anger in check.

John's basketball skills bloomed in high school. But his attitude was still a problem. He talked back to coaches and **referees**. He made angry faces on the bench if he wasn't in the game. After his second year at Garner, John and his family moved to a different part of Raleigh. The move meant John had to switch to Broughton High School. He played well at the Broughton basketball team **tryouts**, but he was cut from the team anyway. Some thought it was because of John's attitude.

Anyone who watched John play saw that he had a special talent for basketball. But his

John ate a lot of junk food when he was young. But his diet changed as he aged. "I eat salads, fruit, salmon, healthy things," he said. "I don't eat fast food anymore."

Broughton High School in Raleigh, North Carolina

anger and bad behavior were holding him back. John realized that he had to change his ways. "Once I figured it out, I just said, 'basketball is my escape,'" he said. "I just . . . basically play every game for [my dad]."

After being cut from the Broughton tryouts, John switched schools again. He went to nearby Word of God Christian Academy. Word of God had fewer than 300 students. John worked closely with the teachers and coaches at his new school. He began treating his teammates and coaches with more respect. Slowly, John's attitude began to change for the better.

At Word of God Christian Academy, John's game improved with his attitude.

College scouts look for the best high school basketball players.

HIS NEW KENTUCKY HOME

In 2007, John played at the Reebok All-American Camp in Philadelphia, Pennsylvania. The camp would give him a chance to show his skills to college **scouts** from all around the United States. Playing college basketball is an important step for athletes who want to play in the NBA someday. John would also have to prove that he could get along with coaches and teammates.

At the camp, John played against some of the top high school players in the country.

In one game, he scored an impressive 28 points. He also proved he had other skills that could make him a top college player. He hit teammates with crisp passes and grabbed **rebounds**. He hustled on defense and worked hard to win every game.

Scouts had been impressed with John's play at the Reebok camp. Some people were even calling him the best high school point guard in the country. As a senior at Word of God in 2008–2009, John strengthened his status as a top player. He scored 22.1 points and snared 5.2 rebounds per game. He also passed for 5.5 assists per game.

As a senior, John worked hard to make himself a better basketball player and teammate.

It was time for John to decide where to go to college. One of the schools he considered was the University of Kentucky (UK). Until 2009, Kentucky coach John Calipari was the men's basketball coach at the University of Memphis. In 2008, Calipari coached Derrick Rose. Like John, Rose is a point guard. After playing just one season with Coach Cal and Memphis, Rose was selected with the first pick of the first round in the 2008 NBA **draft**.

Kentucky has won the National Collegiate Athletic Association (NCAA) championship eight times. Only UCLA, the University of California in Los Angeles, has won more championships (11).

John dreamed of a similar path to the NBA. He announced that he would go to Kentucky. "Coach Calipari pushes his players, and that's why his teams are

John announced with his sister Tonya (*right*) and Dr. Frank Summerfield (*left*) that he would play for Kentucky. Summerfield founded Word of God Christian Academy.

successful," John said. "Some [scouts] compare me to Derrick Rose, and that's a compliment."

In 2009–2010, John and the Kentucky Wildcats had a great season. John scored more than 16 points and passed for more than six assists per game. The team finished with 35 wins and just three losses. That was one of the best records in the NCAA.

John charges up the court with the ball against the West Virginia Mountaineers.

CAPITAL GUARD

At the end of the 2009–2010 season, John and the Wildcats played in the NCAA men's basketball **tournament**. Kentucky was ranked as the top **seed** in their **region**. The team won three games before falling to West Virginia University. John was unhappy with the loss. He had wanted to win the NCAA championship. "We got cut short," he said.

After the season, fans wanted to know if John would return to Kentucky for a second season. Many people expected him to follow Derrick Rose's example and leave for the NBA after one year in college. On April 7, 2010, John and four of his teammates announced that they would enter the 2010 NBA draft. "I'm not the same player as when I arrived at UK," John said. "I believe I'm ready for the next challenge." In June, the draft was held at Madison Square Garden in New York City. The Washington Wizards chose John with the first pick of the first round.

John shakes hands with David Stern, NBA commissioner.

John goes for a layup during the Wizards' 2010–2011 season.

John played well in his first NBA season. He averaged 16.4 points and 8.3 assists per game. But the Wizards did not play well. They finished the 2010–2011 season with a record of 23–59. They played even worse in 2011–2012, finishing 20–46. The team showed slight improvement in 2012–2013 with 29 wins and 53 losses.

Finally, in 2013–2014, Washington played like a top NBA team. John was voted to the NBA All-Star Game, and the team ended the season with a winning record of 44–38. The Wizards made the **playoffs** for the first time since John had joined the team. They beat the Chicago Bulls in the first round before falling to the Indiana Pacers.

John (*second from right, front*) and the Wizards cheer from the bench.

In 2014–2015, John was voted to the NBA All-Star Game for the second time. Fans, players, and coaches knew he had become one of the league's best players. It had been a long journey, but John learned a lot from his rocky path to the top of the NBA. "It made me who I am," he said. "It's why I'm here."

John scored 19 points and added seven assists at the 2015 NBA All-Star Game. But his team lost the game, 163–158.

John dunks the ball during the 2015 All-Star Game.

Selected Career Highlights

2014–2015 Voted to the NBA All-Star Game
for the second time

2013–2014 Voted to the NBA All-Star Game
for the first time
Ranked first in the NBA with
721 assists
Averaged 19.3 points and 8.8
assists per game for the
Wizards
Ranked second in the NBA
in assists per game

2012–2013 Played in only 49 games due to injury
Averaged 18.5 points and 7.6 assists per game for
the Wizards

2011–2012 Averaged 16.3 points and 8 assists per game for
the Wizards
Ranked seventh in the NBA in assists per game

2010–2011 Chosen by the Wizards with the first overall pick in
the NBA draft
Averaged 16.4 points and 8.3 assists per game for
the Wizards
Ranked seventh in the NBA in assists per game

2009–2010 Averaged 16.6 points and 6.5 assists per game for Kentucky
Helped Kentucky win three games in the NCAA tournament
Ranked first in the conference with 241 assists

2008–2009 Averaged 22.1 points and 5.5 assists per game for
Word of God Christian Academy

Glossary

assists: passes to teammates that result in scores

draft: a yearly event in which teams take turns choosing new players from a group

dunk: to slam the ball through the hoop

layup: a shot taken with one hand near the basket

National Collegiate Athletic Association (NCAA): the group that oversees college basketball

overtime: a period of time added onto the end of a game if the score is tied

playoffs: games played to determine a champion

point guard: a player whose main job is usually to set up teammates for baskets with good passes

rebounds: balls grabbed after missed shots

referees: officials in charge of a game

region: one of the four groups of teams that make up the NCAA basketball tournament. The winner of each region plays in the Final Four.

rim: another word for a basketball hoop

scouts: basketball experts who watch players closely to judge their abilities

seed: a number assigned to a team in a tournament that ranks the team based on how likely it is to win

three-point line: a line at both ends of a basketball court. Shots made from behind this line are worth three points.

tournament: a set of games held to decide the best team

tryouts: tests of players' skills. A tryout is held to decide who will become a member of a team and who will be cut.

Further Reading & Websites

Fishman, Jon M. *Derrick Rose*. Minneapolis: Lerner Publications, 2015.

Gitlin, Marty. *Playing Pro Basketball*. Minneapolis: Lerner Publications, 2015.

Kennedy, Mike, and Mark Stewart. *Swish: The Quest for Basketball's Perfect Shot*. Minneapolis: Millbrook Press, 2009.

JohnWall2.com
http://www.johnwall2.com
Visit John's official website for all the latest news, gear, and highlights.

NBA
http://www.nba.com
The NBA's official website provides fans with recent news stories, statistics, biographies of players and coaches, and information about games.

Sports Illustrated Kids
http://www.sikids.com
The *Sports Illustrated Kids* website covers all sports, including basketball.

LERNER
SOURCE

Expand learning beyond the printed book. Download free, complementary educational resources for this book from our website, www.lerneresource.com.

Index

Photo Acknowledgments

The images in this book are used with the permission of: © Patrick Smith/Getty Images, pp. 4, 7, 29; © Brad Mills/USA TODAY Sports, pp. 5, 6; © Tribune Content Agency LLC/Alamy, p. 8; © Brad Mills/USA TODAY Sports, p. 9; © Mlenny/iStockphoto.com, p. 10; © Ethan Hyman/Raleigh News & Observer/MCT via Getty Images, p. 11; © Apostrophe Productions / Exactostock-1598/SuperStock, p. 13; © Jeffrey Camarati, pp. 14, 15; Albertoch90/Wikimedia Commons (CC BY-SA 3.0), p. 17; © Jim Redman/MaxPreps, p. 18; © Chris Williams/Icon Sportswire, pp. 19, 21; AP Photo/Gerry Broome, p. 23; © Chris Chambers/Getty Images, p. 24; © Al Bello/Getty Images, p. 25; © Albert Pena/Icon Sportswire, p. 26; © epa european pressphoto agency bv/Alamy, p. 27; © Kathy Willen/Pool/Getty Images, p. 28.

Cover image: Mark Goldman/Icon Sportswire 749/Newscom.

Main body text set in Caecilia LT Std 55 Roman 16/28.
Typeface provided by Adobe Systems.